The Driver's Guide to
ROAD SIGNS in
FRANCE

A brief guide to the French 'Highway Code':

The rules, road-signs and rights of way

for safer holidays and drama-free journeys..

The DRIVER'S GUIDE to ROAD SIGNS in FRANCE

Contents

	Page
Driving on the Right	4
Road signs in France	7
The red roundel	9
Roundabouts	10
Speed Limits	13
Road Markings	17
Crossroads	19
The French Road Network	21
Auto-routes	22
Routes Nationales	25
Routes Departementales	26
Urban Streets, Parking	28
Don't Forget, Vital numbers	30
Calculator Kph/MPH	34

© Publications
Le Ponteur-Malden
No part of this publication may be reproduced without permission

Introduction.

The 'Code Rousseau de la Route' is the French equivalent to the British Highway Code. We strongly recommend that you do not use this brief English guide merely as a substitute for the real thing; it's best to study the original and adhere to its instructions. The code is available from most newsagents; look out for the sign 'PRESSE' outside the village shop.

As in many countries, the Police have stepped up their campaigns against law breakers on the roads; there are stiff fines for speeding and many radar traps operate. Don't have a long lazy lunch and expect the police to wave you on if you've had a glass or two of wine - they won't. There is a maze of signs in every town, at every junction. One missed sign can cost the inattentive driver dear.

This guide has the driver's – and passenger's – interests at heart. We want you to enjoy France and its wonderful roads and spectacular scenery, so we've provided a condensed version of their Highway Code, to give you the confidence and familiarity to unravel the sometimes confusing French 'way of doing things'. But don't wait until you are in the car.
It's better to study it at your leisure; soon you'll begin to recognise the signs and it will all begin to make sense.

The Authors of this work cannot be held responsible for any incident, accident, fatality, damage, loss or injury suffered on French or Continental roads; we urge the reader to make sure he or she is as familiar with the French Version of the 'Code de la Route' before setting out. This booklet is intended as a short summary and not as a substitute, translation or authorised version of French rules and regulations governing road use.

Driving on the right.

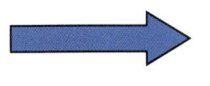

From the first it is important to familiarizes yourself with driving on the 'other' side of the road. Once you've mastered the habit – for that's what it is – it becomes second nature; many drivers can change easily as they change countries. It is certainly easier in a 'left-hand' drive hire car than in your own 'right hand' drive vehicle. A left-hand drive vehicle is (obviously) one with the steering wheel on the left side of the car and the car is driven on the right hand side of the road.

By far the best way of familiarising yourself with the process is to practice 'off-road' if you can, with some cones, a clear open space, without other traffic. Draw a plan of what it's going to look like. If you arrive at an airport with a car hire booked (check position of all the gears, indicators, etc.,) or arrive at a ferry terminal on the other side of the channel with your own car)or a hire car that has a steering wheel in the 'wrong' place), don't venture out into a strange location, instead take a few turns around the car park. Your own (right-hand drive) car will also feel strange, at first, on the 'wrong' side of the road. In a right-hand drive (English) car you'll be next to the kerb. Remember the kerb is your friend – for the rest of your trip it will be your close friend; at every junction, every turn, every manoeuvre, check out of the driver's window that the kerb is next to you.

The best advice for a right-hand drive motorist is – 'don't bother to over-take unless you really have to'. Over-taking is easier with a passenger, but the rule is always; better safe than sorry. Listen to your passengers; if they are nervous from the word go you're probably spoiling their holiday. It's best 'to take a holiday' from the hectic commuting you may be used to; relax, drive slowly, enjoy *your* holiday too.

Even in a hire car, go slowly, take your time. Don't attempt to show local drivers 'how it's done'.

If possible, avoid the National Routes at first, major roads and busy routes. Auto-routes are theoretically easier; it's a simple job to stay in lane and for the right hand drive car the problem of on-coming traffic is eliminated. Difficulties can arise immediately, however, in the form of motorway junctions and entrances and exits. These are sometimes confusing and can appear counterintuitive, with no clear sense of where the Auto-route is heading or which lane to take for your destination.

Use the space available at Auto-route junctions to pull over (before or after the toll) to check the route, the *number* of your next junction. Tolls on Auto-routes are now greatly simplified; almost all accept payment by credit card and most banks don't charge a fee. This saves the search for coins and search for dropped coins. *Slow down well ahead* of the toll booths ('Péage'). Look for the credit card symbol over the marked lanes to the toll booths as you approach and be sure to be in the right lane. Don't pull across lanes at the last minute. Put the card in the slot - ***press the 'ticket' button if you want a receipt - it's a good way of keeping a record of motorways costs-***, within a second or two your card will be returned and when you take it out the barrier will open.

Be careful as you roar away with the others; police check speeds frequently at the 'péages': some fines have been levied to motorists who arrive at the next toll too early! The speed limit is fixed at a maximum of 130Kph in fine dry weather, 110kph if wet or bad visibility.

If you can avoid the 'Routes National' then choose the minor roads (often very direct, good quality and quieter) or the Auto-routes; the 'N' roads (National) are busier and with more speed and traffic checks. These include those based on messages from previous checkpoints (sometimes un-marked police cars) that relay information on speed, phone use, seat belt infractions, etc. It is not the case that police are lenient with foreign drivers, nor that a U.K. registered car is immune from fines, which can be large.

It's best to accept the fact that you are not in your own country and you'll enjoy your driving much more if you don't import all the habits of cut and thrust that you may be used to; drive slowly, considerately and, above all, make use of all the clues available along your route; the road signs.

ROAD SIGNS IN FRANCE....

A few tips that could save a spoiled holiday, a hefty fine or even your life...

Most road signs are self-explanatory and are (more or less) equivalent to British road signs. You'll recognize signs for 'z' bends and a hundred others; symbols for aircraft, pedestrians, children, 'road narrows', lifting bridges, etc., are all contained within the familiar red triangle pointing upwards or a red circle.. These are 'Danger' signs (*panneaux de danger*).

But you won't be familiar with a yellow diamond. Do not ignore this sign.
The yellow diamond signals a change in priority.
Meaning: …..

<u>**You have right of way - but only until the end of the priority section!**</u>

Historically, all traffic from your right had priority on all French roads, everywhere. This custom – the famous 'Priorité à Droite' – still applies, especially in towns, even on some roundabouts. The yellow diamond sign but with a black bar through it, cancels the 'priorité'.

Thus, as a principal route enters a town, built-up area or village, this sign warns you no longer have priority; traffic entering from the right has priority;

   ... **<u>now you must be prepared to give way to traffic from your right</u>**.

Many locals are so accustomed to the rules they will not even glance to their left to see if anything is coming. They simply assume you will follow the Code and give way on the routes in question.

The difficulty is created by the fact that the diamond sign is not a common sight and is on the major routes only; the priority rules rely on the fact that most roads entering from the right have 'Give Way' or 'Stop' signs to prevent traffic from a 'minor' road suddenly entering the traffic flow on a 'major' route.

How do you know that the turning on the right along the road ahead has a stop sign? How do you know if they have priority? If you are on a 'priority route' you can be pretty sure the system works in your favour. 'Pretty sure' is not good enough. You can't tell, so follow this general rule; on major roads, keep an eye out for turnings into the major route entering from the right - look out for the 'end of priority sign' and remember it - assume that in towns and villages priority is from the right and proceed with the necessary caution - your speed should be fifty or less - after the 'welcome' sign into a built-up area, be **extra** careful!

The Red Roundel

Memorise this shape; the red circle means you're in trouble if you ignore it. But what does a red circle (with nothing in it) mean? It means NO CARS from either end of the street - different from no entry. This is French logic at work again; there may be some circumstances in which you might want to find the 'start' of the no entry. This is to tell you 'don't bother': no cars are allowed in the street from any direction
It is also the basic design for all signs that 'forbid' ; basically,

whatever is illustrated in the roundel
is forbidden; caravans, horse, bicycles and just about everything. So the 'no entry sign' in France is more explicit; *'No entry from this direction'*.

"Giratoires" or "Ronde pointe": The Roundabout

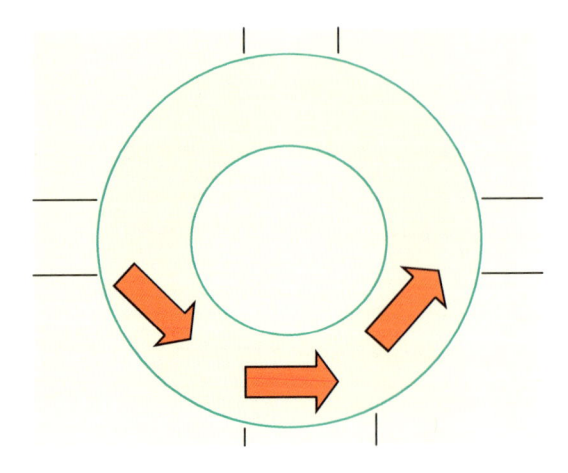

On the 'open road' roundabouts operate (roughly) in the same way as in UK, but instead of operating in a clockwise fashion French 'giratoires' operate in an **anti-clockwise** direction. Remember this simple rule and you shouldn't experience any problems; drive slowly, try and avoid the hectic rush of the local traffic, especially around the 12 noon lunch-break which occurs pretty well instantly all over France.

Traffic load surges sharply as locals try to make it home as quickly as possible. The outskirts of towns, with their relatively new by-passes are full of also relatively new (and often exquisitely decorated) roundabouts. They are also full at peak periods with enthusiastic drivers who have precise knowledge of every curve, passing place and turn off. So enthusiastic that they will often pass and then turn off with superb skill, but often misplaced confidence, right in front of you.

If you are able, much better to find somewhere for lunch and make sure you are off the road at 11.55. As this is usually too early for visitors from the UK, have a strategy ready:

Avoid the routes around local towns at lunchtime by choosing a country route that takes you around the bottle-necks, roundabouts, by-passes. If you are choosing a country route that might take you through towns at peak traffic times, consider timing your journey so that you are on an Auto-route for that stage of your journey.**Be especially careful with roundabouts in major towns and cities: the Priorité rule may still apply, even on roundabouts.**

For example in Paris – on what are, in effect, roundabouts, say encircling a large monument - traffic on the 'roundabout' **gives way** to traffic entering. The sign warning you of this unwelcome fact is by this time perhaps twenty kilometers behind you. Remember, then, that 'Priorité à Droite' is usually to be found entering towns and conurbations and applies even if most of the giratoires you have already negotiated seem to conform to normal logic.

Never assume you have right of way over traffic from the right. Always exercise caution in the above circumstances. Even if local drivers are perhaps, technically at least, in the wrong, you are bound to come of worst. It has to be reiterated that 'Priorité a Droite' is the most difficult problem for the British motorist.

Most roads entering from the right now carry 'stop' signs: a red triangle pointing down with or without the words 'Cedez le Passage' (Give Way). This is also true of giratoires. But you are expected to remember that twenty (or two) kilometres behind you (cancelling the 'priorité' you had got so used to) still has precedence. Remember **French** logic applies, not the version you left behind at the coast.

"Cedez le Passage"
means 'Give Way'

CEDEZ LE PASSAGE

This sign obviously requires a vehicle to yield right of way to vehicles from the left (usually, the 'main' route). This, to many French, is a betrayal of a venerable French custom ('their' priority from the right) and an insult to National Pride.

Beware – on the 'main' route you are on (that may have priority) it impossible to know if the next turning on your right has a 'Cedez le Passage' sign. Beware that you may have missed the Yellow panel declaring that traffic from the right now has priority. Beware also that traffic entering your route from the right is from a track or minor road that has no signs at all. This may occur particularly in towns, small villages, out-of-the-way country roads.

Speed Limits...

.....AND HOW **NOT** TO GET CAUGHT.

An example of what is by far **the most important road sign in France** is shown below.

D 906

COURPIÈRE

Simply a place name? As you enter a city, town or village in France the name of the place greets you. You are expected to know that

<u>as you approach the sign you must slow down to 50Kph</u>.

The road sign that's only a place name is in fact a sign advising you of a speed restriction. Typically, *there is often no advice at this point* of the speed restriction. You are expected to know this vital rule; in built up areas a speed limit applies - your vehicle must be traveling at this speed or less as you pass the sign. *50 Kph* is the rule in all built-up areas.

Many unwary travellers have been caught out by this rule. Often, police radar traps are located just beyond (or sometimes hundreds of yards beyond) the welcome sign informing you that you are about to experience the delights of a pretty village or medieval market town. Chances are, out of view of on-coming traffic, there is a radar detector. An immediate fine is payable, often far more than the price of the pleasant lunch you had been anticipating.

Angouleme, Bordeaux, Corbières, St André, all built-up areas in France have panneaux' (signs) welcoming the unwary driver. But they also welcome, it must be remembered, the safe and considerate driver who's ready to enjoy at leisure the charm of the French urban landscape as well as the rural. Rushing through a town can mean a hefty fine, missing a turning or the opportunity to stop and enjoy what it has to offer.

There are roundels to remind you; 'Rapell' is the word writ large under the speed limit sign when it eventually appears: *remember* !

RAPELL

Fifty km/h is the standard speed for all built up areas, the equivalent of 30 m.p.h. This speed limit is universal in all towns across France **unless otherwise stated.** Sometimes a sign accompanies the town name to remind you of these exceptions. But it is taken for granted that even though no speed limit might have been displayed on the imaginary line you drove across into the built up area your speed should be automatically – even instinctively - reduced. **The town name is the speed limit.**

Here are the most common speed restriction signs: *Ninety Kph* On dual carriageways (non-motorway) and most main roads in non-built up areas.

Fifty Kph. Universal in all 'communes' or administrative are (in reality, small towns, villages, large towns, city districts). The black and white version with the bar cancels the restriction, but only to present you with, often, a different restriction almost immediately.

Seventy Kph: Discretionary in the outskirts of larger towns where roads cater for heavier traffic, also National routes in general.

Lower limits are in place in town and city centres, for areas with 'sleeping policemen' and other traffic calming schemes, smaller towns with narrower streets , etc.

Determined by local conditions, communes may impose 20, 15 or even 10 km/h for schools, pedestrians streets and other hazards.

Rarely, *minimum* speeds apply, (blue background) to prevent slow-moving vehicles causing disruption on through routes. See also auto-routes, below.

Major routes and Auto-routes (motorways):*130Kph* But only in clear weather conditions, dry and with good visibility, un-congested traffic. This is the maximum permitted speed and *only* on auto-routes. In these conditions, use of the outside (left-hand lane) also requires the driver to adhere to a minimum speed of 80 Kph..

In wet weather, fog or other conditions of poor visibility, or heavy traffic conditions (such as in built up areas)

110kph is the maximum speed permitted on Autoroutes. On other major routes such as roads with divided carriageways (but not auto-routes), this is also the top speed permitted.

Approaching tolls or junctions, <u>also the top limit on all other major roads which are otherwise unrestricted:</u> ***90 Kph.***

Thus there are frequent signs restricting speed, for example, 70 or 50 km/h,

depending on conditions and often changing from one to the other within a hundred metres.

Some of the reasoning behind speed restrictions is not always apparent to the motorist. In France the authorities do not make the assumption, often with good reason, that the motorist is a skilled, competent, careful person with other people's safety foremost in his or her mind. Resist the temptation to assume these limits don't also apply to you.

It may be true that coming from Britain you may be an experienced driver used to more 'give and take'. Rest assured, if you take any liberties, especially with speed, you run the risk of being photographed, and – now that traffic violations follow the driver relentlessly to his or her home address – a heavy fine will eventually catch up with you.

ROAD MARKINGS ....
and How to Read Them.
It's all in black and white.

What looks like a simple dotted centre line actually contains important driver information. As if you didn't have enough to do, French road planners have incorporated more road signs into the markings on the road surface.

Whereas upright signs are called in French 'Signalisation vertical', surface markings bear the weighty title 'Signalisation horizontal'. Following inescapable logic a code is written into the white lines. The fact that the inescapable logic doesn't seem to work is borne out by the eye-watering fines that can be levied for infraction.

The most important message for the visiting motorist is a very simple and must seem glaringly obvious:

Never -ever- cross the unbroken white line dividing the carriageway.

That this is regarded as an extremely serious offence may be judged by the penalties handed out; up to a 3 year driving ban and/or 3 points added to you licence. You may see others risking it but be patient; some roads have hidden dips or unseen junctions.

If there's a broken white line, notice that these are of different types; long intervals between the dashes ('guidance' type) means overtaking is permitted given the usual caution necessary; short intervals ('dissuasion' type) indicates that sometimes slow traffic is common (farm vehicles, for example) or that the road itself requires greater attention because of curves, dips or change of surface. Thus, short dashes are **not** an invitation to overtake, but to exercise caution.

Further coding is embedded in the lines at junctions; a continuous line from the centre to the curb emphatically means 'Stop'. A stop signs reinforces the fact that you shouldn't 'creep' over the junction, even though you can see nothing is coming. You have to physically stop the vehicle.

A dotted or broken line means you can proceed with caution but that you don't have priority. As mentioned previously, in small villages, urban centres and the like, "Priorité à Droite" may apply. There may be no line at the junction you arrive at. To be on the safe side, treat these junctions, even if you are the beneficiary of the priority system, as if they had a dotted line across them: proceed slowly, keep a good look out.

You cannot be fined for driving slowly and with care out of a turning providing you have physically stopped the vehicle and made sure the way is clear. On the other hand, you can cause a major mishap by trying to be 'too French' and treating these markings as if they don't apply to you personally.

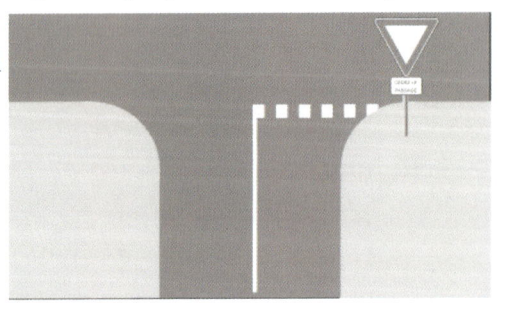

Notice the difference in the schemes for these two road junctions; one has an imperative 'Stop' sign (octagonal) and solid white line. The other (Cedez le Passage or 'Give Way') has a broken white line and inverted triangle to indicate a warning and caution. You may see the latter at Giratoires (roundabouts). Road markings have their own special language.

Crossroads

By now the reader will have realised there is more to French road signs than meets the eye; it's easy to miss the surface markings and even some of the 'Vertical Signalisations' – the 'upright' signs.

These can come into play even on what seems to be the quietest country lane. For example, small white vertical posts with a red band mark a crossing or access road of equal status with regard to priority. Approach such crossings with caution; another driver (even another 'foreigner') may be bowling along a clear, straight country road making good time. On a rapidly closing course – your potential collision speed is a sum of the speeds of both cars – you may hesitate to make a decision; "Surely, it's my right of way?"

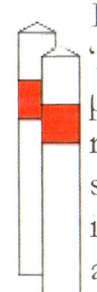

Is it ? No – and this applies to both drivers. The 'Balise' – four upright markers – display the position of an intersection, especially on rural roads. Given the vast nearly flat stretches of some of the French countryside, it is sometimes impossible to clearly see that another road is about to cross the one you are following.

Watch out for these markers and act accordingly.

There are usually four but they themselves give no indication of priority – often this is 'priorité à droite'. There is no harm in slowing down to make sure, rather than finding out - too late – that the other driver thinks he can beat you to it, even if *you* have priority.

Many crossroads forewarn drivers about distance to the crossing and right of way but on rural routes it is *un*likely that you'll find a clear indication that the route you are following has priority:

The sign with a broad vertical arrow indicates to the driver that priority is in favour of the traffic on that road.

The alternative indication of a crossroads is a simple diagonal cross, indicating that neither route has priority, so 'priority a droite' will apply. Obviously, this simple cross sign is the most important one to recognize and remember!

It's easy to confuse these signs – they both indicate 'crossroads' – but in the second case no reminder is given of priority to traffic from the right. For the local driver it's a matter of custom, habit and instinct.

With luck, you may have advance warning, but France is a big country with hundreds of thousands of kilometers of roads, so here the priority rule makes sense.

But be prepared to slow down and give way. Never be

tempted to speed up and race for a junction. It's a hundred percent certain the other driver is thinking exactly the same thing.

The French Road Network

Auto-routes - The main interconnecting motorway system.

Routes Nationales — Long distance non-motorway routes.

Routes Departementales — local roads.

Auto-routes

France has an enviable system of high quality, well maintained and – in general immaculate motorways.

Any decent map will give an overall picture of the extent and coverage of the motorway system; any in-car navigation set will provide a easy an effective way of negotiating them. Such a system usually includes motorway 'aires' or rest areas, which often include good quality restaurants and cafés as well as service stations. The larger establishments often have two or three different eating venues, from snack bars to quite elaborate restaurants.

On an auto-route the traveller can cover long distances, often gaining a good overall impression of the countryside and a true sense of the scale and variety of the France as a whole. But be sure to take into account the cost of the auto-route tolls as part of the of your holiday or business trip.

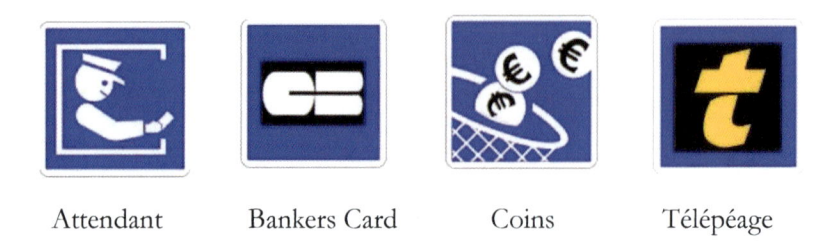

| Attendant | Bankers Card | Coins | Télépéage |

The toll booths are mostly automatic and accept credit cards, without the need to key in numbers. The process is quick and painless and the machines will give receipts, useful for keeping a check on your travel costs. Most banks do not charge a fee for this type of payment at toll booths.

Another service is available that makes the already efficient toll system even easier; Télépéage is a method of paying without stopping. An electronic card in your car automatically makes the payment as you drive through a special 'Télépéage' lane. Speed has to be below 30 km/h. The payment is made direct from your bank. Cards are available for frequent users of the auto-route, such as business travellers, etc., but holiday-makers with some understanding of the language can arrange for the use of a temporary card that's available for one month. You'll find this service on the internet at vinci-autoroutes.com/telepeage.

As with any journey it's best, of course, to have a plan of action and this should contain the identifying numbers of the junctions important to your trip; names of local towns may override important destinations you may be on the lookout for and the destination town you were hoping to see may not appear on the overhead signs. The junction numbers are consistent and, in the long run, more reliable.

There are advance warning of junctions ahead. If there's an important intersection of motorways on your route check your sat-nav or map in an 'aire' rather than on the road. Such intersections sometimes seem interminable, especially in large cities where 'périphériques' are involved; these are the auto-route 'ring roads' that take you around large conurbations. Often these are crowded with local traffic and speed limits apply. These are always well signed.

'Périphériques' are usually allocated one of two names – 'interieur' and 'exterieur'. In effect, they form a large roundabout with 'interieur' traffic heading along the clockwise motorway that circles the city and 'exterieur' traffic heading anticlockwise. All that's necessary is to identify the number of the junction you need. As many turn-offs near a city may be close together on an auto-route périphérique you may need a larger scale map or sat-nav to provide the right information. Note also that some new roads recently connected to périphérique may have resulted in some junctions being labelled (for example), first, junction 10a and the next, 10b. Be certain (some prior planning needed here) which is the one you want.

Radar traps are fairly frequent on auto-routes, especially on those tempting sections where you feel you can make us some time without anyone noticing. *Unfortunately*, the police have much more experience than the average motorist in this line of work. There are cameras hidden on bridges or live patrols with radar equipped binoculars, unmarked police cars and pairs of motorcycle patrolmen connected to the radio network.

Better to relax and enjoy the countryside.

Because of their international connections, auto-routes generally have internationally recognised signs. There may be some signs unfamiliar to British visitors especially those advising of approaching tolls. These are logical; their purpose is to reduce the speed of oncoming traffic through a series of signs, complete with flashing reminders. There will almost certainly be police lurking somewhere near.

The vast expanse of road can be confusing, so it's best to pick a suitable toll booth some way out: look for the symbols denoting cash with attendant, credit card, Télépéage, etc., and head slowly and steadily for it. Try to remain unmoved by the fact that an adjacent lane suddenly seems emptier. Swapping lanes can land you in trouble. Concentrate instead on getting away slowly, smoothly and unscathed (apart from the amount of the auto-route toll). **NOTE:** As a visitor, it's really not worth worrying about coins; the right money is best, though change will be given, but at an inconvenient, even inaccessible, slot at the bottom of the machine. Occasionally there is a price displayed ahead of the barrier, but it's never far enough ahead. Unless you are very relaxed and immune to the scale of the queue that can build up in just a few short minutes, the toll booth is an uncomfortable place to sort through slippery and indecipherable Euros. Pay by card but make sure beforehand that your bank does not charge a handling fee for auto-route toll transactions.

Most other signs on the auto-route are self-explanatory but do take note of them, especially when four lanes of traffic travelling at high speed have to merge.

ROUTES NATIONALS

These routes connect most large towns and conurbations. They carry both commercial traffic and private cars that are either going between local centres or avoiding adding further costs to a longer journey. Additionally, they offer far more opportunity to stop when necessary or change from one route to another.

They also, of course connect with minor roads. Thus, the 'N' roads are more demanding, with cross roads and intersections, restrictions in towns and villages. If they by-pass built up centres then there are myriad intersections and roundabouts. Mostly these intersections are well signed, but make one mistake and getting back on route is sometimes difficult; local signs ignore the fact that your journey is concerned with destinations with which the locals have little or no concern.

The way out of this is to follow the signs that say 'Autres Directions'. Annoyingly, these signed routes can take you all the way around a town, so avoid this strategy at all costs in somewhere like Paris! In smaller towns you will (eventually) come back to the sing you are looking for or (worst case scenario) the place where you first took the wrong turn. But if you are exploring France, the Routes Nationales are the classic choice. They've even written songs about them; the route 'National Seven' ends up in St Tropez.

Because of their variety and complexity they are heavily policed. Speed limits come and go with dizzying regularity. Instances of Priorité à Droite sections are still common and the yellow diamond is your cue to become even more alert.

The 'N' road system is inextricably linked to the Michelin

maps, once the bible of the French traveller. Towns or villages underlined in red on these maps are featured in the famous Michelin Guide – the 'red' guide. An advantage therefore of travelling the Nationales is that the true dimensions of France open up in a way that the auto-routes cannot offer; wine regions, cultural and historic centres, architecture, gastronomy, as well a the unique atmosphere of each City, town and village, greets the traveller.

The message here is clear; if you don't have to cover long distances in a hurry, despite the extra effort the 'N' roads have a great deal to offer, especially if you acquire English versions of the Michelin Guide (red) and the regional guide (green) that will enhance the experience of driving the roads of France a hundred fold.

ROUTES DEPARTEMENTALS

In general, these roads are the responsibility of local Departments. In rural areas they offer real delights and can lead you to all but undiscovered territory. You'll need good maps, preferably Michelin, or sat-nav, a room already booked somewhere, a full fuel tank, bottle drinks and a picnic basket. The sad fact is that most smaller villages are bereft of shops, tabacs, bars, boulangeries, filling stations, bistros or hotels. Though these small communities were once the life blood of France and still reflect the variety and scope of French culture and history, many have moved to the conurbations where the schools and supermarkets are to be found, the offices and businesses.

This leaves the countryside in many departments quiet, free of traffic, calm and undisturbed. The traveller is able to roam and dawdle at leisure, especially if the school holidays are over.

For the driver these roads (coloured yellow on Michelin)

can also prove to be an advantageous way of cutting across country; many head - unswervingly - for miles towards the horizon offering surprisingly direct and relatively effortless travel.

There are a few points to be aware of – see the section above on 'Crossroads' and watch out for the four white posts with red markings. Theses are mostly plastic and some may be missing. There are other minor hazards such as agricultural traffic; this varies according to season. On mountain roads in Spring and late autumn you may find yourself caught up in the 'transhumance'. Hundreds of sheep and goats, sometimes thousands, take over entire districts as they are driven on foot to and from the highland pastures.

In early summer on the plains huge combine harvesters cut maize or cereals; these monsters can take up the whole width of a road. In September and October the Vendanges (the wine harvest) fills minor roads with helpers, tractors and trailers, tankers and lorries.

Temporary signs may be put up and its best to exercise caution; for example, the 'fauchage' sign warns you that the commune whose road you're using is cutting the grass verges, sometimes with two tractors, one for each side of the road. Don't be impatient – they will have seen you, despite every indication to the contrary.

You may also see, during Autumn and Winter, signs warning that 'La Chasse' (hunting) is underway. There will be dogs, men, four-by-fours and sometimes the kill at the side of the road. The attention of the participants is by no means concerned with traffic, though these events are usually well organised and well signed (orange triangles).

In general country roads will take you into the heart of France – with some local produce in your picnic these well kept and often beautiful roads are not to be missed.

Urban Streets and Town Driving

Most road signs will be familiar, stopping and parking is a little more complicated.

In some streets one side only is for parking. Perversely, this changes according to days of the month – the 1st to the 15th of the month on one side, then 16th to the end of the month on the other. So you need a knowledge of the calendar and how many days there are in the current month. These figures are printed in white on a blue circle within the inevitable red

No stopping (ever).   No Parking.   Park only according to date *

*Parking on one or either side of a street: - 1.15 means the 1st fortnight the month, 16.31means the second fortnight.

This system is further complicated by other instructions denoted by arrows underneath the roundel. A left pointing arrow means no parking in that direction, right pointing arrow means no parking in that direction. Thus there are also signs with up or down arrows meaning no parking after (up) or before (down) the sign. Various other added panels indicate other restrictions, but theses are easily decipherable.

Practically all other signs are decipherable to the British driver. Well, mostly ...

…..this one means the driver coming from the direction of the red arrow must give way to 'white'. In English it's called a 'give way' sign. In French ;

«Priorité par rapport à la circulation venant en sens inverse ».

Some parking zones are 'blue' zones. Parking is free but limited in time. In these areas a blue disc within a 'wallet' with windows to show the time you arrived is placed so as to be clearly visible (pavement side) for inspection. These discs are adjusted by the driver and are purchased for a small fee in the 'Presse' (newsagent). Parking meters list the time limits and costs in other parking zones. These 'horodateurs' (parking meters) should not be ignored.

One main problem with urban centres is the plethora of signs; driving slowly and carefully is sometimes hard as the driver gets caught up in the traffic 'flow'. Signs can be missed or only glimpsed. One useful strategy is to consciously recognise from the start that mistakes are inevitable, that it's no great loss to stop and get your bearings. If unsure at a round about, just go round again, or as many times as it takes to find the right road.

"Ask a policeman" is not always possible - they are mostly travelling by car. But pedestrians are only to wiling to assist if you have the name of a main town on your route. Be careful when listening to their response; don't mistake "tout droit" (straight on) for "a droite" (to the right)– this can cause untold confusion, so confirm what you've understood with some gallic arm waving in the direction necessary. "A gauche' (to the left, or turn left) is easier to understand.

Part of your strategy – one that can add enjoyable zest to your travels – is to embrace getting lost as part of the whole experience. It's in these circumstances that you may well meet people or encounter events, sight, sounds, and adventures that provide the memories you'll treasure. Don't be afraid - now you know what to look for – to park the car, find a cafe, sit and relax and watch the world go by. You've probably earned a decent break by now. Towns often hide a covered market. Ask a local – you'll be astonished at the variety of produce on offer (the French are eternally and justifiably proud of their produce).

DON'T FORGET....

With this small but important guide, much of the mystery of the French roads can be unravelled, especially when read in conjunction with the original 'Code de la Route'. You'll add to your confidence, too, by making sure you have in your car all the proper equipment legally required for driving in France, in addition to your personal papers, licence, insurance and photocopy of your the log book:

Two warning triangles, spare set of bulbs, high visibility jacket , inflated spare tyre in good condition, surgical gloves, breath test kit, first aid kit.

Be aware that alcohol limits are now very low in France - 0.50g/l. (UK 80 g/l) Any (even apparently minor) accident may involve the police carrying out breath tests. Use of drugs is similarly outlawed, as are mobile 'phone use (even with a hands-free kit), eating and smoking, anything, in fact, that materially interferes with the drivers concentration.

Fines are heavy and swiftly imposed 'on the spot' for traffic offences such as speeding or crossing an unbroken white line (see above) or pulling over onto an auto-route 'hard-shoulder' without indisputable cause, driving without a seat belt. Don't judge local attitudes and behaviour as the bench mark to follow; the French drivers are often at fault and should not be regarded as models to imitate. Here are some sobering facts to take into account.

France is roughly twice the size of UK with a similar population.
Accidents per thousand vehicles for both countries are as follows; Britain 3.1 per 1,000 vehicles, France 6.1 . This despite the fact that, theoretically, France has much more road space, which begs the question 'why do they drive so close to the vehicle in front?', and why are their road accident statistics among the worst in Europe, worse even than Italy?

Plenty of additional information is available from :
Foreign and Commonwealth Office, AA and RAC and on-line.
To make sure your visit is enjoyable, gather as much information as you can before setting out. Make this part of the experience, adding to your store of knowledge and honing your expertise.

With all this accomplished you'll be sure to enjoy...

Driving the Roads of France – Bon Route!

> **In your car you must carry:**
> Two warning triangles, spare set of bulbs, high visibility jacket, inflated spare tyre in good condition, legally-approved breath-test kit, first-aid kit, GB sticker (fitted), headlight beam adapters, original licence and log book,
> insurance.

With this small but important guide, much of the mystery of the French roads can be
unravelled.

Bon Route!

ROUTE PLANNER

Towns	Road Number	Junction Number

Remember:
France is roughly twice the size of UK
with a similar population.
Accidents per thousand vehicles
for both countries are as follows;
Britain 3.1 per 1,000 vehicles, France 6.1 .

CALCULATOR

KMPH		MPH
10	=	6.21
20	=	12.43
30	=	18.64
40	=	24.85
50	=	31.07
60	=	37.25
70	=	43.50
80	=	49.71
90	=	55.92
100	=	62.13
110	=	68.35
120	=	70.56
130	=	80.78

(Tip: if it doesn't obscure the speedometer, use a small piece of red adhesive insulation tape to physically mark the position of the relevant Kph equivalents).

IMPORTANT PHONE NUMBERS

Emergency Numbers
EMERGENCY: 112
(Europe wide and for mobile phones)

France: Emergency   112
Medical (SAMU)   15
Police (Gendarmes) 17

British Embassy and Consular Offices

Paris - British Embassy, 35 Rue Du Faubourg St. Honoré, 75363 Paris, Cedex 08 Paris. Tel: (33) 144 51 31 00

British Consular Office, 353 Bvd. President Wilson, 33073 Bordeaux.Tel: (33) (5) 57 22 21 10

British Consular Office, 24 Av. De Prado, 13006 Marseille Tel: (33) (0)491 15 72 10

Other personal or important numbers before you travel ?

------------------------------------   -----------

" **The Essential In-Car Guide for Anyone Traveling to France …** "

- Auto-routes & 'Péages'
- Road Signs
- 'Priorité a Droite' Rules
- Speed Limits
- Parking in Towns
- Emergency Numbers
- Breath Tests
- Legal Requirements
- Kilometre Conversion Chart
- The French Highway Code
- In-car Kit
- Consular Contact

© Publications
Le Ponteur-Malden
A Division of Meridian East Ltd.
leponteur-malden@gmail.com

Printed in Great Britain
by Amazon